Martial Arts for Women

MARTIAL AND FIGHTING ARTS SERIES

Judo
Jujutsu
Karate
Kickboxing
Kung Fu
Martial Arts for Athletic Conditioning
Martial Arts for Children
Martial Arts for the Mind
Martial Arts for People with Disabilities
Martial Arts for Special Forces
Martial Arts for Women
Ninjutsu
Taekwondo

Martial Arts for Women

ERIC CHALINE

Senior Consultant Editor
Aidan Trimble (6th Dan)
Former World, European, and
British Karate Champion
Chairman and Chief Instructor to the
Federation of Shotokan Karate

MASON CREST PUBLISHERS
www.masoncrest.com

Mason Crest Publishers Inc.
370 Reed Road
Broomall, PA, 19008
(866) MCP-BOOK (toll free)
www.masoncrest.com

First printing

1 2 3 4 5 6 7 8 9 10

Library of Congress Cataloging-in-Publication Data on file at the Library of Congress

ISBN 1-59084-395-9

Editorial and design by
Amber Books Ltd.
Bradley's Close
74–77 White Lion Street
London N1 9PF
www.amberbooks.co.uk

Project Editor Chris Stone
Design www.stylus-design.com
Picture Research Lisa Wren

Color reproduction by MRM Graphics, England
Printed and bound in Jordan

IMPORTANT NOTICE
The techniques and information described in this publication are for use in dire circumstances only where the safety of the individual is at risk. Accordingly, the publisher and copyright owner cannot accept any responsibility for any prosecution or proceedings brought or instituted against any person or body as a result of the use or misuse of the techniques and information within.

Picture Credits
Paul Clifton: 13, 18, 29, 87.
Nathan Johnson: 17.
Sporting Pictures: 8, 11, 14, 20, 23, 40, 46, 56, 68, 82, 85.
Bob Willingham: 6, 26, 38, 57, 58, 62, 70.

Front cover image: Paul Clifton

Contents

Introduction

When I began studying the martial arts back in 1972, the whole subject was shrouded in mystery; indeed, that was part of the attraction. At that time there was only a limited range of books on the subject and therefore very little information was available to the novice.

I am glad to say that this has changed in recent years beyond all recognition. With the explosion of interest in the martial arts and the vast array of quality books that are now on the market, we seem to be increasing our knowledge and understanding of the martial arts and sports science, and this fact is reflected in this new series of books.

Over the past 30 years, I have been privileged to compete, train, and teach with practitioners from most of the disciplines covered in this series. I have coached world champions, developed and adapted training methods for people with disabilities, and instructed members of the armed forces in close-quarter techniques. I can warmly recommend this series as a rich source of information for students and instructors alike. Books can never replace a good instructor and club, but the student who does not study when the training is finished will never progress.

Aidan Trimble—Sixth Dan, Former World Karate Champion

Although women are, on average, smaller and weaker than men, and carry less muscle mass, they can become formidable opponents once they have been schooled in the martial arts.

Women's Health and Fitness

For centuries, Western women were taught that they were the "weaker sex." It was thought "unladylike" for women to excel at any physical skill more demanding than needlework. It is not surprising, therefore, that when it came to self-defense, women were considered helpless victims who looked to their male partners and kinfolk for protection.

Fitness training and sports are no longer considered out of bounds for women, but there are still differences in the activities that men and women do. Go to any sports club and you will see more men in the gym pumping iron and more women in the dance studios, doing aerobics and step classes. Even on the sports field, sexual **segregation** is taking its time to disappear: men have their sports (football, boxing, and baseball), and women have theirs (volleyball, field hockey, and synchronized swimming).

The martial arts are no exception to this rule. When they became popular in the 1970s, promoted by television series such as *Kung Fu* and films such as *Enter the Dragon* (which featured the famous martial artist Bruce Lee), they attracted mainly male participants because of their macho image.

Women have played a growing role in the martial arts since World War II, not only as students, but also as competitors and teachers. Once directed into the defensive arts, such as aikido and t'ai chi ch'uan, women now regularly compete in contact karate and taekwondo tournaments.

WARNING

Although all the fitness techniques shown in this book are safe for an average fit person who has properly warmed up (see pp. 19–25), any exercise is potentially hazardous for a beginner, who may not be aware of how far to push him- or herself. You should, as a matter of course, always consult your doctor before beginning a new type of exercise. He or she will no doubt encourage you, but may have special advice for you if you suffer from high or low blood pressure, diabetes, or if you are pregnant. Should you feel any dizziness, acute pain, or excessive tiredness while performing any of the techniques or drills in this book, stop immediately and seek medical advice.

In the martial arts, however, size and strength are not the determining factors in who is going to win a **bout**. With two equally skilled players, the stronger one will no doubt have the advantage. However, if a beginner, no matter how strong or large, were to be pitted against a smaller, weaker, but more advanced student, the beginner would find him- or herself lying flat on his or her back, wondering what had happened.

TIME, PLACE, CLOTHING, AND EQUIPMENT

One of the advantages of the unarmed martial arts styles (as opposed to armed martial arts such as **ninjutsu**) is that their practice requires little or no equipment. The place of practice is, however, important. Both in their daily lives and when training in the martial arts, the Chinese place great importance on environmental conditions. Rules about where and when it is best to live, work, and train have been codified into the art known as **feng shui.**

Feng shui is a complex subject, but suffice to say that when training, just let common sense be your guide. For example, if you wish to train outdoors, choose firm land that is sheltered from the wind. Training is best done in the morning, when the body and mind are rested. Avoid training on a full stomach (wait at least two hours after a heavy meal), but a light meal or snack before training is recommended so that it provides you with the energy to exercise without weighing you down.

The Chinese do not encourage the display of the human body, in part for moral reasons, and also because of health concerns. When training, you should wear loose-fitting clothing, such as a t-shirt, sweatshirt, or track-suit. Wear clothing that is appropriate to the season, layering in cold weather so that you can remove and replace layers as your body warms up and cools down.

While the Japanese train barefoot, the Chinese use flat-soled cloth slippers that give the foot some basic protection while providing a firm footing. Avoid training shoes with such thick soles that they will prevent you from feeling

Sexual segregation is still apparent in Western fitness, where weight-training is still preponderantly male and aerobics classes are still a largely female activity.

the ground beneath your feet. Avoid running shoes as well, as they are designed for stability while jogging or running, and provide little or no lateral support.

The aim of any fitness program is to develop muscular strength, aerobic (heart-lung) fitness, and flexibility. The Western approach is to treat these goals as separate, with specialized activities for each: weight-training for strength; cycling, running, or aerobic dance for heart-lung fitness; and stretching or yoga for flexibility. Unless you are practicing a sport, little or no attention is paid to the other components of fitness, such as balance, posture, or coordination.

The martial arts' approach is quite different. Although martial artists perform strengthening exercises, like push-ups and sit-ups, as well as stamina-building exercises such as running, these exercises occupy a small part of the overall training. The bulk of training is in the technique of the art itself.

As you proceed in the martial arts, your fitness will improve as a natural consequence of performing the techniques correctly. This not only includes strength, stamina, and flexibility, but also other skills, such as balance, coordination, and agility. But there is still more: a factor that the Chinese call qi, or **chi**. According to Chinese philosophy, chi is the force that animates the cosmos; without chi, there would be no life. A full understanding of the martial arts of China, Korea, and Japan is not possible without an appreciation of the concept of chi.

Training in the martial arts also differs from Western fitness in that no matter how proficient you become, there is always another level toward which to aim. While runners and weight trainers will learn one set of

Training for health and fitness varies widely between East and West. In the West, there are specialized exercises for strength, stamina, and flexibility, while in the East, the martial arts provide an integrated approach to fitness.

techniques, which they will practice with little variation for the rest of their training careers, martial artists can progress to more and more complicated techniques in their arts, or learn new fighting styles.

A BRIEF HISTORY OF CHINA'S MARTIAL ARTS

The Chinese "hard," or "external," fighting arts that we know as **kung fu** have their origins in the teachings of a sixth-century Indian Buddhist monk named Bodhidharma (Tamo in Chinese). Bodhidharma traveled from India to China to teach a new form of Buddhism that would one day become Zen Buddhism in Japan. After a meeting with the Chinese emperor in 520 B.C., Bodhidharma retired to the Shaolin monastery, where he found the monks to be holy in mind, but extremely weak in body. He taught them a series of exercises to enable them to meditate for long periods of time. Over the next thousand years, these simple techniques were developed into the **shaolin lohan** fighting system.

In 1674, the **Ch'ing** Emperor, K'ang Hsi, fearing that the monks had become too powerful, ordered that the Shaolin temple be destroyed and its monks slaughtered. Only five monks and nuns managed to escape the destruction, and each went on to found their own styles of Shaolin kung fu.

Najinata players in action. In Japan, the wives of samurai learned to fight with the sword, staff, and spear, just like their husbands.

FEMALE FIGHTERS

It is only in the Western world that women have been considered helpless victims, incapable of defending themselves. Asian women, by contrast (though they have the reputation of being submissive), have fought alongside their men, using many of the same fighting arts. In fact, women have created several martial arts, including **wing chun** in China and **pentjak-silat** in Indonesia.

A woman named Yim Wing Chun created the wing chun style. After the destruction of the Shaolin monastery, a nun named Ng Mui fled to the southern province of **Fujian** and later to **Yunan**. One day, she met a young woman called Yim Wing Chun, whose name means "Beautiful Spring." According to the most popular version of the legend, Wing Chun was the daughter of a merchant by the name of Yim Shee. Wing Chun attracted the attention of a local official, who wanted to marry her. When she turned him down, the suitor jailed her father.

Wing Chun ran away and asked Ng Mui to train her in the martial arts. When she came back to the village, she announced that it was impossible for her to marry a man who was not her equal in combat. Amused, the official agreed to meet her in combat. She defeated the official, but in his rage, he had his men kill her father. Wing Chun escaped the official's fury and became a rebel, fighting against the reign of the Ch'ing Dynasty.

Ng Mui had trained Wing Chun in the "plum flower fist" style, which Wing Chun eventually decided was better suited to men. She then created her own style, which she dedicated to Ng Mui, but named after herself.

The legend behind the Indonesian art of pentjak-silat tells the story of a village woman who had gone down to the river to fetch water. While there, she witnessed a fight between a tiger and a giant bird. She watched the two animals fight for several hours, until both died. When her husband, who had come to look for her, tried to hit her for being away from home so long, she evaded his blows easily by using the techniques she had just witnessed.

In Japan, the wives and daughters of **samurai** warriors were sometimes called away to fight alongside their husbands, or to defend themselves in the absence of their husbands. These women were trained in **naginatajustu** (the art of the halberd). The **naginata** is a spear-like weapon with an axe-shaped blade, which gave women the extra reach they needed against a swordsman.

Perhaps the most famous female martial artists from Japan were the **kunoichi** (female **ninja**), who were trained in the same deadly armed and unarmed fighting techniques as their male colleagues.

WHICH MARTIAL ART?

There are hundreds of martial arts to choose from, from the well-known Japanese and Chinese arts, to the relative newcomers from Brazil, Thailand, and Indonesia. These arts can be divided into offensive and defensive styles, and also into "hard/external" and "soft/internal" styles.

The classical example of an offensive, hard/external art is Japanese karate ("the art of the empty hand"). Karate employs the brute strength of bone and muscle in a style that can best be summed up by the saying, "The best defense is a great offense." At the other end of the spectrum is an art like

BREAKING STEREOTYPES

Western women, if they have been encouraged to train in the martial arts at all, have typically been directed toward the defensive, soft/internal arts. Although it is true that strength and size are less important in these arts—and that agility and flexibility are important—there is no reason why women should be limited to them. The choice as to which type of martial art to practice should be made on the basis of your own temperament, along with your physical aptitude.

Teaching styles vary between the Japanese and Chinese martial arts. The Japanese are much more regimented, using standardized clothing and examinations, while the Chinese teaching method is more individualistic and fluid.

t'ai chi ch'uan ("great ultimate fist"), a defensive, soft/internal art that makes use of both the practitioner's chi and the attacker's own energy to deflect an attack.

Teaching styles vary widely in the martial arts. The Japanese and Korean arts have a formal, regimented style, with regular exams, internationally recognized grades, and strict etiquette concerning clothing and behavior in the **dojo** (training hall). In contrast, the teaching style of the Chinese arts is more individualized and less structured. This style has its own drawbacks, however, as you can never be sure of the authenticity of the qualifications of a kung fu master. When choosing a teacher, go to the recognized national or international body regulating his or her art, and find out whether he or she has an approved qualification.

Warm-Up and Preparation

Women have the advantage over men when it comes to flexibility due to a combination of physiological and social factors. Women need more flexible joints for childbirth, and they are also more likely to take part in activities that develop flexibility, such as dance.

Regardless of this advantage, the need for a thorough warm-up before any form of exercise, no matter how gentle the exercise may appear, cannot be overstated. Many sports injuries can be avoided with only a few minutes of limbering up. The frequent kicks and rapid changes of direction that are found in many martial arts are demanding on the joints, especially the knees and the spine, so particular attention should be paid to warming up these areas.

There is no single standard way of warming up, but the general rule is to move and loosen up all the major joints and muscle groups of the body. The main joints are the wrists, elbows, shoulders, ankles, knees, hips, and most importantly, the spine, which is the largest joint in the body. The major muscle groups are the hamstrings and quadriceps, the large bundles of muscles at the front and rear of the thighs (these muscles

Like aerobic dance, training in the martial arts is fast-paced and demands high levels of flexibility. A thorough warm-up is essential to avoid injury and to increase the effectiveness of the workout.

Apart from contact injuries from stray blows and kicks, the martial artist is vulnerable to abrasion injuries from falls, and to more serious damage to the joints, in particular, the knees, lower back, and shoulders.

are particularly vulnerable to tears and sprains when not properly warmed up); the calves; the tendon that attaches your heel to your calf (called the Achilles tendon); and the muscles of the arms, shoulders, back, and chest.

SHORT WARM-UP PROGRAM

Refer to the time, place, and clothing guidelines in the introduction before performing the warm-up sequence. This particular routine is based on Chinese exercises known as qi gung (see next chapter, p. 27).

SOME BENEFITS OF WARMING UP

Many people imagine that a five-minute warm-up on a running machine or a stationary bicycle is sufficient. While this will get the pulse rate up, the blood pumping, and the leg muscles and joints warm, it does not really warm up the spine or the upper-body joints and muscles. A good warm-up will give you the following important benefits:

• Increases blood supply to the muscles
• Irrigates (oils) the joints
• Raises the pulse rate
• Prepares the mind
• Mobilizes the chi
• Protects against injuries

HEAD ROLLING

Begin your warm-up program with a head-rolling exercise. Stand in a relaxed position with your feet shoulder-width apart, your hands hanging loosely by your sides, and your back and head erect. Drop your head to the left, and tilt it so that you are looking at your left shoulder. Slowly roll your head forward to the center, and then around, until you are looking at your right shoulder. Move slowly and smoothly, deepening the movement with each roll. Reverse the direction back to the left. Repeat five times in each direction.

A brief warning when doing this exercise: Even if you have no history of back or neck problems, do not go beyond your shoulders and tip your head backwards, as this will put pressure on your fragile cervical (neck) vertebrae.

SHOULDER ROLLS

Stand in a relaxed position with your feet shoulder-width apart, your arms hanging loosely by your sides, and your back and head erect. Shrug your shoulders as high and as far forward as they will go, bringing your shoulder blades up and together. Now roll your shoulders back as far as they will go, and then lower, then depressing your shoulder blades and spreading your shoulders wide. Circle around until you are back at the starting position. Repeat at least five times, slowly and smoothly, before reversing the direction for a further five rolls. Keep the arms soft throughout, and do not heave them up as you roll your shoulders.

WAIST ROTATIONS

These are also beneficial. Stand in a relaxed position with your feet hip-width apart, your arms hanging loosely by your sides, and your back and

Many people think a quick jog or stationary cycle is a sufficient warm up, but in the martial arts, it is vital to warm up all the body's joints and major muscle groups, both in the upper and lower body.

head erect. Begin turning from the waist slowly and smoothly, letting your arms move freely. Increase the momentum gradually, and let your arms slap into your body with each turn. Turn from the waist, not from the shoulders. Everything below your waist should be still, and everything above it should move as a single unit. Complete at least 10 rotations in each direction.

KNEE CIRCLES

These are another important warm-up exercise. Stand with your legs and feet together. Bend your knees, and rest your hands on your thighs. Begin making small circles with your knees in one direction, gradually increasing the size of the circle over at least 10 circles. Repeat for at least 10 circles in the opposite direction.

A brief warning when doing this exercise: Your knee and ankle joints are fragile structures when pressure is applied against their planes of movement. The knee, for example, will be injured if too much pressure is applied from the side. The martial arts can be demanding on the knees, with their low stances, rapid changes of direction, and kicking techniques. Thus, care should be taken to warm up and stretch the legs thoroughly.

BASIC STRETCHING PROGRAM

Stretching builds on the effects of the warm-up. Although the following exercises are not drawn specifically from the martial arts' traditions, martial artists use them as part of their daily routine.

HAMSTRING STRETCH

To perform the hamstring stretch, stand with your feet about shoulder-width apart. Take a step forward with your right leg. Keeping both legs straight and both feet flat on the ground, bend forwards from the waist, as if you were trying to touch your knees with your chin. Put both hands on your leading leg, for stability. Hold for five breaths, pushing a little further each time you exhale. Repeat for another five breaths with the left leg leading.

QUADRICEPS STRETCH

You may wish to use a chair or wall for support during this exercise. Stand with your legs together. Bend your right knee, and grab your right ankle with your right hand. Keeping your knees together, pull the right leg behind you as high up as it will go. Hold for five breaths, pulling a little higher each time you exhale. Repeat with the left leg.

CALVES STRETCH

For this exercise, which stretches the calves, you may want to use a chair or wall for support. Stand with your legs together, and then take a long step forward (like a lunge). Keeping your head back, your rear knee straight, and your back foot on the ground, push forward from your hips. You should feel a strong stretch in your lower leg. Hold for five breaths, pushing each time you exhale. Repeat with the other leg.

A brief warning when doing this exercise: Do not let your leading (bent) knee go over and beyond your toes, as this can put undue strain on the joint. Your knee should form a right angle.

TRICEPS STRETCH

To perform the triceps stretch, stand in a relaxed position with your feet apart. Raise your right arm straight up, and then bend it at the elbow, so that your hand is behind your head. Take hold of your right elbow with your left hand. Pull toward the left while bending to the left from the waist. Hold for five breaths, and repeat on the other side.

BICEPS STRETCH

You will also need to stretch your biceps. Stand in a relaxed position with your feet about shoulder-width apart. Keeping your head and back erect and your arms straight, flex your wrists so that your palms are facing the floor, with your fingers pointing forward. Slowly push your arms straight back without bending your elbows.

Hold this position for five breaths, pushing a little further back each time you exhale.

Energy Work

To the Chinese, one of the intangible benefits of training in the martial arts is known as chi. As we have seen, the ancient Chinese believed chi is the force that animates the cosmos, without which there would be no movement or life.

According to the ancient Chinese, chi is found in the environment all around us and within our own bodies. It drives the blood through our arteries and provides the spark that gives life to our muscles and brains. We take in chi whenever we eat and breathe, and we can also pick it up from the cosmos itself (if we are correctly attuned to it). Imbalances in bodily chi can make us ill and must be adjusted by taking herbs, or by inserting needles into invisible channels known as the **meridians** (chi flows through the body along the meridians according to the teachings of the art of acupuncture).

If chi is freely available, the ancient Chinese reasoned, then it might be possible to increase its store in the body and thereby improve health and prolong life. Over two-and a-half millennia, Chinese doctors refined a series of techniques to manipulate chi that included diet, medical treatments, and physical exercises, which were known as **qi gung**.

At some point, the Chinese realized that if chi could be used beneficially to heal, it might also be used to injure. The fighting arts that use chi in this

The Chinese increase and manipulate chi by using a combination of physical posture, breathing, movement, and the power of the mind to maintain health and prolong life. Both physical and mental strength is essential in this regard.

way are called "soft," or "internal," arts, to differentiate them from the "hard," or "external," arts that rely on the strength and hitting power of bone and muscle.

Of all the internal arts, t'ai chi ch'uan, or t'ai chi, is the best known in the West, where it is often taught as a relaxation and health-promoting exercise. T'ai chi ch'uan, however, is actually an awesome martial killing art. Unlike shaolin lohan and many other Chinese martial arts, t'ai chi is not connected with Buddhism, but with China's other great religion, Daoism (also known as Taoism). One of the legends about t'ai chi's origins relates that the 13th-century Daoist monk, Chang San Feng, learned its techniques from a god in a dream.

The basic t'ai chi techniques are contained in "the form," a set sequence of exercises that are typically performed in slow motion. Each style of t'ai chi has its own version of "the form"; these versions vary in length from 24 movements to over 100. The Chinese government created the **Simplified Beijing Form**, taking elements from several of the existing t'ai chi forms. This composite form is now practiced as a health and fitness exercise routine by millions all over China.

The two other arts usually classed along with t'ai chi as internal are **hsing-i**, which uses circular motions based on the eight **trigrams** of the **I-Ching** (Book of Changes), and **pa-kua**, which has the reputation of being one of the more difficult of the internal arts. Unlike the circular motions of t'ai chi and hsing-i, pa-kua is linear—that is, the movements are conducted in straight lines. T'ai chi also teaches armed fighting technique forms, which involve the sword and the spear.

The t'ai chi form can itself be categorized as qi gung, as one of its main functions is to increase the amount of chi at the practitioner's disposal. T'ai chi also seeks to enable its practitioners to move chi in and out of their bodies. The t'ai chi form is too complex a subject to deal with in a book of this scope, but we will look at the "raising chi" exercise, which begins the form, followed by a series of qi gung exercises.

The postures of t'ai chi ch'uan were modeled on the movements of real and mythical animals, such as the monkey and dragon.

RAISING CHI

Stand with your feet parallel and hip-width apart. Your knees should be soft, and your head and back straight, but your shoulders should be relaxed and your chest should be sunken (rather than puffed out).

A common description of the ideal t'ai chi stance is that of an infant in his or her first years of walking, before stress and bad posture begin to affect the way he or she walks and stands. Your head should be balanced on top of your spine, without falling forwards and rounding your upper back; your stomach muscles should be firm, but not clenched (and you should not be holding your stomach in);

RAISING CHI

STEP 1: Stand with your feet shoulder-width apart, hands by your sides, fingers together, palms facing backward, knees soft.

STEP 2: Bend your knees and breathe in as you raise your hands slowly to chest height. The arms remain relaxed and slightly bent.

and your lower back should be naturally curved, but not hyperextended (so that your buttocks stick out). Your arms should hang down at your sides.

Once you are settled into this posture, focus your attention on a point two inches (5 cm) below your navel. The Chinese call this point the **dantian**, and believe it is one of the main energy reservoirs in the body. Chi stored in the dantian, it is believed, can be redirected at will to other parts of the

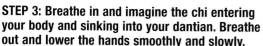

STEP 3: Breathe in and imagine the chi entering your body and sinking into your dantian. Breathe out and lower the hands smoothly and slowly.

STEP 4: As your hands reach the starting position, straighten your legs. Repeat 10 times, drawing the chi with your mind into your dantian.

body. Keeping your focus in the dantian, begin to deepen and even out your breathing, so that your inhalations and exhalations are of the same length. Breathe more deeply than usual, but do not strain or force the air in or out by using your stomach muscles.

Once you have counted 10 slow breaths, breathe in and turn your arms so that your palms face behind you. The fingers and thumb are aligned, but still relaxed (you are not making a karate-chop hand). Exhale, and allow your hands to return to their natural hanging position. On the next inhalation, turn your arms and palms again, and raise your hands a couple of inches more. Continue raising your hands a little further each time you inhale, until they reach chest level.

Your arms and hands should be completely relaxed, with the joints fully open to allow the free flow of chi. Your hands should float up and down smoothly and slowly, as if they were in water. Once you are comfortable with this exercise, breathing in and out as you raise and lower your arms, return your focus to the dantian.

Imagine that chi is entering your body with each breath, like an insubstantial, luminous fluid. While the air goes into your lungs, the heavier chi sinks into your dantian, where it accumulates. You may experience a warming of the body and some tingling in your hands, both of which are natural effects of this exercise.

QI GUNG

Ancient Chinese medical practitioners developed the qi gung exercises over thousands of years. They used them to treat all ailments from the common cold to diabetes, as well as to improve general health and fitness. The exercises given here will increase and balance the flow of chi in your body, and also have specific benefits on your lower back as well as your metabolic functions.

AUTOMATIC MOVEMENT EXERCISE

The following exercise demonstrates the power of chi to move the body

ROWING THE BOAT

STEP 1: Stand with your feet shoulder-width apart, your knees soft, and your arms by your sides. Breathe in.

STEP 2: Draw your arms back and up, making large circles with your hands.

STEP 3: Breathe out and bend forward as your hands come around and down. Keep your arms straight and your palms facing downward.

STEP 4: Straighten your body as you draw back your arms until you are in the starting position.

LOOKING AT THE MOON

STEP 1: Stand with your feet shoulder-width apart, your knees soft, and your arms by your sides. Turning your body, shift your weight to your left foot and bring your right foot to its toes. Breathe in as you swing both arms up and to the left.

STEP 2: Bend your right elbow, and position your right hand so that the palm is facing up; the left palm should be facing down. Breathe out as you bend your knees, turn your waist to the center, and lower your arms.

STEP 3: Repeat the movement turning to the right, breathing in as your body rises and out as it is lowered.

SCOOPING THE SEA

STEP 1: Stand with your feet shoulder-width apart, your knees soft, and your arms by your sides. Breathe out. Take a step forward with your left foot, and shift your weight onto it; your right knee should be straight, with the foot on the floor. Stretch your arms out in front of you.

STEP 2: Lean forward, bringing your hands together and ahead of your left knee. Bend your knee further, but do not allow it to go over the toes of your left foot.

STEP 3: Breathe in as you begin to shift your weight back from your left to your right foot. Open and draw back your arms.

STEP 4: Look up as you open your arms wide. Return to the starting position and repeat with the right leg.

ROTATING WHEEL

STEP 1: Stand with your feet slightly wider than shoulder-width apart. Your feet should be turned out, with your arms resting by your sides.

STEP 2: Breathe out as you bend forward, supporting yourself with your hands on your thighs. Your fingers should point inward.

independently of the conscious mind. You should perform this exercise in an open area that is clear of any obstacles.

Stand in a relaxed position with your feet shoulder-width apart. Take several deep breaths to clear your mind, and focus on the dantian. Tap your navel with the fingers of your right hand, and rub the top of your head with the fingers of your left hand. Then perform six to nine repetitions of three of the qi gung exercises detailed above.

When you have finished, stand still and imagine the chi flowing down

STEP 3: Without raising your body, turn to the left from your waist until you have completed a full circle.

STEP 4: Breathe in as you complete the circle, and then return to the starting position. Repeat the exercise, turning to the right.

from your head and up from your feet. Allow your body to move freely, but remember that your movements can become expansive and dynamic. If the exercise is done correctly, you can begin to move at quite a pace with your arms and legs swinging widely.

As you do not direct the movement consciously but let the chi control your body, this can be disturbing to a beginner. If you become worried about this, reassert control over your body by focusing your mind on stillness, and gently stop moving.

Muscular Endurance

The way that you stand and hold your body—your stance and posture—is often overlooked in Western training and sports, but it is one of the fundamentals of martial arts training. In the offensive martial arts, such as karate and shaolin lohan, the basic stances are the first techniques taught.

Stance is a fundamental part of any martial art. It determines both your balance and reach in an encounter, and also how much of your body is exposed to an attacker's strikes. If you stand squarely facing your opponent, for example, you are presenting a much larger target than if you were standing at a 45-degree angle.

Training in stances can also be used to improve your fitness. Holding low stances will develop muscular strength and endurance in the legs. It is surprising how short a time a beginner can hold a one-legged stance before he or she falters. Correct stances promote good posture, another important aspect of fitness that is often overlooked. The dynamic stance and "push hands" exercises (see pp. 43–45) develop balance, speed, and coordination in equal measure.

The foundations of all the martial arts styles are their basic stances. A proper stance alone can decide whether you will win or lose in an encounter. In this forward stance, the martial artist shows her determination to vanquish her opponent.

Stances are also important in armed martial arts styles of combat, such as kendo (fencing), kyudo (archery), and bojutsu (staff), shown here. These women will alter their stances frequently during the course of combat, depending on the moves of their opponent.

HORSE STANCE

Stand with your feet together and your arms by your sides. Turn your feet so that your toes point out to the sides, and then turn your heels out so that your toes are pointing inward. Repeat the two movements, and then turn your heels so that your feet are parallel to one another. Your feet should now be at the correct width for the stance. Make fists with your hands, and bring them to your hips. Your weight should be evenly distributed on both feet and your buttocks tucked in under you, as if you were sitting down. Do not allow your knees to go over your toes, as this will cause strain on the joints.

FRONT STANCE

Stand with your feet shoulder-width apart. Imagine that there are two parallel lines running through your feet. Take a long step, with the toes of your right foot pointing forward on the right imaginary line. Your left foot should remain on the left line; you may wish to turn it out slightly to maintain your balance. Your weight should be distributed 60 percent on the front foot, and 40 percent on the rear foot. Your back and head should be upright, and your hips square. Hold your hands on your hips, as in the horse stance.

REAR STANCE

Stand with your feet shoulder-width apart. Imagining a line that runs through the center of your body, take a step back so that both of your feet are on the line. Point your front foot forward, and bend your leading leg at the knee. Turn your rear foot out for support, and bend your rear knee. Your weight should be 30 percent on your front leg, and 70 percent on your rear leg. Your torso should be upright, but turned to 45 degrees rather than facing straight on. Hold your hands on your hips, as in the horse stance.

ONE-LEG STANCE

Stand with your feet together. Bend your left knee as you lift your right foot, and put it down in front of you, resting on the ball of your foot or off

STANCES

HORSE STANCE: With your weight evenly distributed on both feet, bend your knees low, and tuck in your seat.

FRONT STANCE: Keep the body upright with 60 percent of the weight on the front leg. Make sure the knee does not go beyond the toes.

REAR STANCE: The feet are on the same line, with 70 percent of your weight over the back knee.

ONE-LEG STANCE: Lift your foot off the floor, or rest it on the ground without putting any weight on it.

the ground. Your weight should be entirely supported by your bent rear leg, so that you can lift your front foot without losing your balance. Hold your body and head erect, and hold your hands on your hips, as in the horse stance; you could also adopt the Chinese "playing the lute" hand position. If your right foot is leading, hold your right arm out in front of you, with your palm facing inward and the left arm bent. Your left palm should be facing your right elbow. This looks more like playing the harp, but it is called "playing the lute." If your right foot is leading, hold your right arm out in front of you, with your palm facing inward and the left arm bent. Your left palm should be facing your right elbow.

Stance exercises are the fundamental training techniques in the martial arts, beginning with holding the stances to develop strength and endurance in the legs, and majoring to dynamic stance work to improve balance, agility, and speed.

HOLDING STANCES

Starting with the horse stance, hold each of the stances described for between one and five minutes. Alternate putting your legs in the front and rear positions. As your legs become stronger, deepen the depth of the stances and increase the time that you hold them.

DYNAMIC STANCES

Imagine that you are standing with your feet together on a clock face, with twelve o'clock in front, six o'clock behind, three o'clock to the right, and nine o'clock to the left. Move from one stance to the next (horse right, horse left, front right, front left, for example), going around the clock face. Start

PUSH HANDS

STEP 1: Stand away from your partner in a front stance, with your right arm extended at chest height. Your partner stands in rear stance with his right hand extended.

STEP 2: Begin to circle slowly, starting the movement in the waist. The feet do not move. Keep low on bent knees.

slowly, building up speed until you have done every stance in all four directions. Once you are familiar with the stances, you can change the order and directions, choosing more challenging patterns.

PUSH HANDS

"Push hands" is a practical application of stances taken from t'ai chi. Another function of this exercise is to feel your partner's chi as he or she moves with you. The aim is to find any point at which your partner is rigid or unbalanced, and then tip him or her over using minimal pressure (just enough to make him or her falter).

STEP 3: You do not put any pressure in your hands and your body should be completely relaxed. You are trying to "read" your partner's energy.

STEP 4: If you feel your partner stiffening at any moment, you can use that stiffness to overbalance him.

Stand about three feet (about one meter) from your partner in a low front stance. He or she should mirror your position in front of you. Hold out your hand in front of you at chest height. Make contact with your partner's hand, but do not put any strength into your touch. Maintaining contact with your partner's hand at all times, begin to circle slowly, shifting your weight from the front foot to the rear foot (into rear stance). Turn from the waist as you circle—not from the shoulders. Move slowly and smoothly, and try to remain at the same height. If you looked at people doing push hands from above, they would be making a figure 8 pattern. The feet, however, do not move.

Strength and Stamina

The drills in this section serve two purposes. First, by learning and practicing the techniques, you will improve your stamina, speed, and coordination. Second, they will prepare you for an actual combat situation in which you have to strike an attacker with one or more of your own "deadly weapons"—your hands, feet, elbows, or knees.

The Japanese word **kata**, meaning "form," is used to describe a set of graded sequences in the art of karate. In the extremely structured and formal Japanese teaching environment, **karate-ka** (those who practice karate) progress from simple to more complex kata as they advance through the rankings.

Karate has its origins in Okinawa, an island south of Japan. The Japanese invaded Okinawa in 1609, and immediately banned anyone from carrying weapons in order to snuff out the possibility of any armed resistance. What they had not counted on, however, was that the islanders had learned unarmed fighting techniques from their Chinese neighbors. They put up stiff resistance, using an art that was then known as **Okinawate** (Okinawa hand). They also turned agricultural implements, such as the **tonfa** (the

Full-contact hard-style martial arts, such as karate, are extremely dangerous sports. In competition, protective gear is used to avoid injury. When learning moves, the students practice them against an imaginary opponent in the kata sequences.

THE ART OF KARATE

Karate training develops great physical strength and stamina through intense training in kata and kumite (non-contact sparring). Like other martial arts, the basic fighting strategy of the art can be summed up by the adage, "The best defense is offense." The karate-ka makes devastating use of his or her natural weapons to deliver killing blows against an opponent's most vulnerable spots.

handle of a rice grinder) and the **kama** (a sickle) into makeshift weapons. The Japanese responded by forbidding the study and practice of the island's native martial arts. The islanders, however, continued to study and develop Okinawate in secret.

Over the centuries, the islanders accepted Japanese rule, but it was not until the beginning of the 20th century that the Japanese authorities recognized the value of Okinawate as a sporting discipline. In 1912, a young schoolteacher named Funakoshi Gichin gave a demonstration of Okinawate to a visiting admiral of the Imperial Japanese Navy. The admiral was so impressed that a few years later, Funakoshi was invited to Tokyo to give a demonstration in front of the emperor. He went on to open the first karate dojo in mainland Japan, called the **Shotokan**. Okinawate was renamed karate-do (the way of the empty hand), and remains one of the more popular styles of karate in the world. Other teachers followed Funakoshi to Japan to teach other styles of Okinawate, and several of Funakoshi's senior disciples went on to found their own karate schools and styles.

KATA

The following exercises are based on karate kata training, which develops both muscular strength and aerobic fitness. They build on the stances detailed in the previous section, so make sure you are familiar with the four

LUNGE PUNCH

STEP 1: Start in front stance with your left foot leading and your left arm extended in a fist in front of you.

STEP 2: Step forward into a right front stance, and punch with your right fist while pulling back your left fist to your hip.

basic stances before beginning this section. Be sure to follow the warm-up guidelines (see pp. 19–25) before attempting any kata drills.

The basic components of the kata are punches, blocks, and kicks. When practicing the techniques, imagine that you are fighting an imaginary attacker, and target specific parts of his or her anatomy with your strikes. Vary the height of the delivery of your punches and kicks; they can be high (**jodan**), to the face; middle (**chudan**), to the torso; or low (**gedan**), to the groin or lower stomach.

Never practice with a live partner, as any mistakes will be costly. Once you have learned the techniques, you may want to practice on a punching bag, but start soft and slow, as a mistimed kick can lead to a broken toe.

Every fighting style in the world counts the basic punch with the fist (also known as forefist in karate-do) as one of its techniques. The martial arts, however, have refined the basic punch in which one straightens the arm to connect with the target; they have added a rotation of the forearm and a coordinated rotation of the hips to increase the power of the punch.

LUNGE PUNCH

To perform the lunge punch (junzuki), start in a front stance, (see p. 41) with your left foot leading, your right hand in a fist on your hip, and your left hand extended straight out in front of you, also making a fist. Bring your right foot forward so that it passes close to your left foot, which turns out slightly. Your right foot continues forward, forming a forward stance. As you shift your weight onto your right foot, snap your left fist back to your hip, and simultaneously punch with your right fist. Rotate both fists at the end of the movement. Your hips should end facing forward squarely, with your feet hip-width apart, and with 60 percent of your weight on the front foot.

REVERSE PUNCH

For the reverse punch (gyaku-uzuki), stand in a left front stance. Punch once, so that your hands are now in the correct position (your right hand at your hip and your left arm outstretched). Turn your left foot out, and slide your right foot past it. As you complete the step, draw back your leading fist and punch with the other one, rotating both as you strike. Your hips should end facing forward squarely, with your feet hip-width apart, and with 60 percent of your weight on the front foot.

FRONT KICK

This kick (maegeri) begins in a modified front stance, with your left leg leading, so that

REVERSE PUNCH

STEP 1: Start from a left front stance, but with the right fist extended and the left at your hip.

STEP 2: Step forward and simultaneously punch with your left fist and pull back with your right.

STEP 3: Finish in a right front stance, rotating both fists as they hit the imaginary target.

FRONT AND BACK KICKS

STEP 1: Standing in front stance, lift the foot, sole down.

STEP 2: Once your knee is as high as it will go, extend the leg to strike.

STEP 1: Standing in rear left stance facing your imaginary opponent, turn to the right.

STEP 2: Shift the weight to the left foot and kick straight back with the right heel.

your legs are hip-width apart. For this kick, your weight should be evenly distributed on both feet (rather than 60/40, as in the regular front stance). The modified element of this stance refers to your arm position. Your arms are in front of you in a defensive posture: your left fist at chest height with the elbow bent, and your right fist at stomach height. Bring your arms back, turn your left foot in slightly, shift your weight onto it, and lift your right foot off the ground. Do not lift the foot heel first; lift it up flat. Lift your knee as high as it will go (it is meant to reach your opponent's head), and extend your leg forward. Aim to strike the target with the large, fleshy pad just under your toes. Lower the leg into a right forward stance, with your arms as before, but with the right arm leading.

BACK KICK

For the back kick (ushirogeri), begin in a rear stance (see p. 41), facing your imaginary opponent. Then shift your weight onto your bent rear right knee and turn your body to the right, stepping onto your right foot. As you shift your weight onto the left foot, your back is turned on your opponent. Lift your right foot and thrust it backwards in a straight line, heel first, into your imaginary opponent. Drop your leg as if you were performing a turn, and return to a rear stance.

SIDE KICK

The side kick (yokogeri) begins in a horse stance (see p. 40), with the weight equally on both feet. Lean to your left, shifting your weight onto your left foot, and raise your right knee. Twist slightly on your left leg as you thrust the side of your foot at your imaginary opponent.

SIDE KICK

STEP 1: Starting in horse stance, lean to the left and raise your right knee.

STEP 2: Extend the right leg to strike with the side of your foot.

ROUNDHOUSE KICK

For the roundhouse kick (mawashigeri), begin from a left modified front stance, turn your shoulders to the left, and lift your right foot. With your hips following your shoulders, turn your supporting foot counterclockwise about 60 degrees. Bring your knee across the front of your body as you continue rotating your hips. Strike your imaginary opponent with your instep (the top of your foot). Place your foot down into a new modified front stance.

DRILLS

Martial arts training uses repetition drills to enable the student to respond to attacks without having to think about his or her response. The more you drill, the better your "body memory" of the movement or technique will be.

The first drill begins in the horse stance (see p. 40). Standing in a low, wide stance, punch alternately with your fists, drawing the other hand back to the hip. Remember to rotate the fists. Perform 20 strikes with each fist. In the next drill, you will practice punching techniques. In an open area, perform both punches (see pp. 49 and 50) on the move (that is, throwing punches while stepping). Do at least 20 punches, 10 with each fist. A good way to practice kicking techniques is to do at least 20 of the four kicks (see

ROUNDHOUSE KICK

STEP 1: Starting from a left front stance, turn to the left and raise your right foot.

STEP 2: Bring your foot across your body to strike with your instep.

pp. 52–55), standing in the appropriate stance. The rear, front, and roundhouse kicks should be performed on the move.

Once you are familiar with the punches and kicks, ask a partner to throw a soft object (an inflatable beach ball, a cushion, or a pillow) randomly at your body or head at various heights. Choose the most effective movement

The kick powered by the largest muscles and the largest bones in your body is one of your most devastating self-defense options. Good stance, giving you stability and leverage, is vital in performing an effective kick.

from your repertory of punches or kicks to repel the object. Once you have practiced the drill without an object in a stationary position, ask your partner to begin circling you. Shift from stance to stance preparing to repulse your partner's attacks.

COMBINATIONS

Once you are confident performing the punches and kicks, both standing and on the move, you can begin to combine them with one another, as a karate-ka would in the various kata. Here are some of the most basic combinations: front kick followed by a reverse punch; front kick, roundhouse kick, then a reverse punch; roundhouse kick, back kick, then a reverse punch. Practice these combinations until you are comfortable with them, and then create your own. Your combinations can also include blocking techniques.

Drills work on the repetition principle: after many repetitions, any movement or sequence will become automatic. We use this learning technique extensively in everyday life to acquire skills such as driving and typing.

Self-Defense

Every manual on self-defense stresses that if you can avoid a fight, you should. Only fight as a last resort. After all, if someone wants to rob you of your money, cellular phone, or shopping bags, these items are certainly not worth risking serious injury—or even death.

If you ever find yourself in a situation in which you have to defend yourself physically, there are a number of options for dealing with potentially dangerous situations. The first option is to escape: Run first and ask questions later. The second option is to give in. If your attacker is only interested in robbing you, then give him or her what he or she wants. The third option is to hit and run. If your attacker is overconfident and has let down his or her guard, or if you think you can take him or her on, use a striking technique against a vulnerable target spot that will disable or slow him or her down, and then run away. The fourth option is to "go for the kill." In situations of extreme danger, when you feel your life is being threatened and you fear pursuit, you can use multiple strikes to the attacker's vulnerable spots.

THE LAW

The rights to defend your physical person and your property are fundamental human rights, and are enshrined in the constitutions and legal

Wearing the right clothes is an important factor in self-defense. In a street situation, high heels may compromise your balance, and tight clothing will restrict your freedom of movement. Martial artists practice these techniques wearing loose-fitting clothing, as shown.

AN ARMED ATTACKER

When faced with an armed attacker, you should always either run or give in. An attacker armed with a baseball bat will have a longer reach than you, and he or she can strike you without getting into the range of your techniques. If faced with a knife-wielding attacker, attempt to improvise a weapon or shield of your own—the lid of a garbage can or a length of wood, for example. And remember, no one, not even famed martial artist Bruce Lee, is faster than a bullet.

systems of all liberal democracies. The U.S. Constitution goes as far as giving its citizens the right to bear arms (specifically guns) to defend themselves.

However, your right to self protection is limited by the concept of using "reasonable force" when dealing with a potential threat. While it might be acceptable to injure an attacker who is in the process of attacking you, it is not acceptable to injure someone who only looks as if he or she might be about to. The law protects the rights of every citizen—even those of the criminal—and it is sometimes the case that the victim ends up being charged as the assailant.

BREATHE, RELAX, AND DROP

When attacked or threatened, a common reaction is to panic, triggering a crisis reaction. Breathing becomes shallow or stops altogether, sapping your energy; your muscles contract, making your body stiff and raising your center of gravity, thus making you an easy target; and your mind goes blank, making you the perfect victim.

If you feel the panic syndrome setting in when in a dangerous situation, go through the "B-R-D" routine. The "B" is for "breathe"; this part of the routine involves getting your breathing under control. Breathe deeply and slowly. This will slow down your heartbeat and give you back control over your mind and body.

The "R" is for "relax"; in this part of the routine, you consciously relax any tension in your body, especially around the neck, shoulders, and chest. If you strike a punch when you are stiff, you will lose your balance. Moreover, if you are relaxed, you have a better chance of avoiding a blow.

The "D" is for "drop"; in this final part of the routine, you position yourself low into the rear or front stance, with your hands up, protecting your face and body. This will immediately improve your balance (when your weight is evenly distributed on both legs, you are easier to knock over). Being in this stance will make you a more difficult target to hit, and might even make your attacker reconsider his or her intentions when he or she sees you in a martial arts fighting stance.

TARGETS

The human body can withstand terrible punishment and, at the same time, be extremely fragile. Bruce Lee, who was a superbly trained martial artist, died because a mistimed blow caused a fatal internal hemorrhage.

You could pummel a male attacker's chest, upper arms, or any area covered by a thick layer of muscle without causing any serious injury or pain. Hit him just hard enough in a vulnerable spot, however, and he may pass out, be in too much pain to continue the attack, or even be permanently injured.

Targets have to be selected with care. You may want to prevent someone from pursuing you, in which case you should go for the knee or the instep; or you may want to knock your attacker out cold, in which case you should go for targets on the head or the neck.

Contrary to popular belief, a man's groin is not the best target. For one thing, a male attacker is very conscious of his weakness there, and thus may be on his guard for such an obvious attack. Furthermore, a mistimed or obvious kick to the groin might result in you finding yourself hopping on one leg as your attacker catches hold of your foot. As well, when compared to the

Multiple opponents do not always present an insuperable problem to the trained martial artist. When faced with multiple assailants in a street situation, you should quickly identify who is the greater threat and tackle him or her first.

neck, head, or rib cage, the groin is a relatively small target. Finally, everybody has a different pain threshold, and so even a kick or punch that connects may not cause enough pain to discourage your attacker; it may just make him mad.

INJURY PREVENTION

Sprained and broken limbs, cuts, scrapes, and concussions can result from falls no higher than from a pair of high heels. No matter which self-defense techniques you know, they will be useless if you are lying stunned, injured, or unconscious on the ground. This section will teach you how to fall safely or roll out of harm's way.

If you manage to fall down unhurt, the ground is not always such a bad place to be. Your legs are the strongest muscles in your body and have a great deal more reach then your arms. If you have sturdy shoes on, your feet will be protected. Moreover, the assailant will be standing above you, leaning forward and potentially off balance. Several prime target spots are within range of your feet: your attacker's groin, inner thighs, knees, and shins.

Another aspect of injury protection is to block an attacker's blow so that it is deflected harmlessly, giving you an opening for your own strike.

BREAK-FALLS

The techniques in this section are taken from the Japanese arts of judo ("the way of suppleness") and aikido ("the way of harmony"). Both of these arts, which are relatively recent creations, look back to the far older martial art of jujutsu ("the compliant art") as their common ancestor. Jujutsu is Japan's original martial art, and was used by the samurai and ninja in unarmed combat. Influenced by Chinese martial art styles, it employs a blend of striking and throwing techniques, as well as joint locks and strangles. Kano Jigoro, the founder of judo, and Ueshiba Morihei, the founder of aikido, were both jujutsu masters.

Judo and aikido are sometimes called Japan's "soft" arts, but they are quite different from China's internal arts, t'ai chi, hsing-i, and pa-kua. While the Chinese arts are based on striking techniques, both judo and aikido use throws to deflect or neutralize an opponent's attack, and joint locks, hold-downs, and strangles to control him or her. There are no kata in judo and aikido; students learn new techniques from the teacher and practice them during free-sparring sessions. Students progress through the rankings by taking regular grading exams, during which they demonstrate their mastery of progressively more difficult techniques. Practitioners develop high degrees of flexibility, balance, coordination, speed, and stamina.

In contrast to karate-do, judo and aikido are defensive arts. As in jujutsu, the basic principle of these arts is to use the opponent's own strength against him or her. Size and brute strength, therefore, are not always advantages in judo, particularly in aikido. For example, it is an aikido cliché in Japan for the large hulking Western beginner to be paired with a much smaller, demure Japanese girl, who proceeds to thrash him and throw him around the dojo.

The way to succeed in break-falls is to start slow, small, and low, gradually increasing the height, range, and speed of the movement. Begin your practice on something soft: a layer of cushions or a mattress, for example. In judo and aikido dojos, the flexible wooden floor is covered in **tatami** mats (mats made of woven rice straw). These mats provide a firm surface, but are also yielding, like thick turf. You should practice break-falls in every direction in which you are likely to fall: forwards, backwards, and to both sides.

BACKWARDS BREAK-FALL

Squat at the edge of your padded training area, with your head tucked in and your arms crossed at chest height. Make sure your mouth and teeth are closed to avoid any biting injuries. Round your spine, and let yourself roll back until your shoulders are on the floor. As you feel your shoulders come into contact with the floor, slap the ground with your palms and forearms at a 45-degree angle to your body; this action will stop your backward momentum and absorb the impact. Once you are at ease with this technique, try it out on the carpet. Begin to gradually increase the height from which you fall until you are standing upright and can fall back without hitting your head. With time and repeated practice, you will find that your body will learn and internalize the action.

BACKWARDS BREAK-FALL

STEP 1: Squat on the edge of a padded surface. Tuck your head and arms in.

STEP 2: Allow yourself to fall back, keeping your back rounded.

STEP 3: As your shoulders touch the floor, slap the ground with your hands and forearms.

SIDEWAYS BREAK-FALL

STEP 1: Starting low, break your own balance so you fall sideways.

STEP 2: Keep your head turned away from the direction of the fall.

STEP 3: Slap the floor with your palm and forearm as your shoulder touches the floor.

SIDEWAYS BREAK-FALL

Tuck your head into the shoulder that is opposite to the direction of the fall. Cross your leg to break your own balance, and allow yourself to fall to the side. Slap the mattress or floor with your palm and forearm; ensuring that your arm (not your body) absorbs the energy of the fall. The timing of the slap is crucial: It should come just as the shoulder hits the floor. Slap too early, and you may injure your arms; slap too late, and you may injure your shoulder. As with the backwards break-fall, start in a low squatting position on a padded surface before attempting the standing version.

FORWARDS BREAK-FALL

This is a jujutsu technique. Begin in a low crouching position on a padded surface. You then dive forward onto your palms and forearms, allowing your elbows to give under your weight.

ROLLOUT

An alternative to the forwards break-fall is the aikido rollout. When falling forward, reach out and form a circle with your arms. Tuck your head in, roll over your arms and back, and return to the standing position.

DRILLS

Beginners in judo, aikido, and jujutsu are repeatedly drilled in break-falls and rollouts until they are completely comfortable with them and they become an automatic response. During free sparring, there is no time to think "I am being thrown, I need to perform a break-fall or rollout." In a surprise attack, there is even less time to think ahead and plan a response.

To perform a sideways break-fall drill, move the length of a room or a pre-set distance outdoors using sideways break-falls, alternating between the right and the left. Perform at least 10 break-falls in

ROLLOUT

STEP 1: Fall forward, forming a circle with your arms.

STEP 2: Roll on your shoulders and upper back.

STEP 3: Your momentum should get you up to standing.

each direction. To perform a rollout drill, move over the same distance using the aikido rollout. While it is easy to progress down a dojo rolling out or break-falling from side to side, it is not possible to do so with front or back break-falls. These are much rarer. The student should be encouraged to dive to the side or rollout when struck or thrown, as he or she will be ready to get up and respond.

BLOCKS

The first approach to blocking an incoming punch or grab is to hit it hard with your forefist or dominant hand. You may hurt your attacker—even break his or her arm—but you will not necessarily disable him or her. The second option is to **parry** the blow by redirecting it. This action gives you a chance to

A block can be used to deflect an attacker intent on grabbing your arm or clothing to pull ʹou in toward him. A well-delivered blow delivered with a fist or sword hand can break a ʹrson's forearm.

BLOCKING EXERCISE

You can practice blocking by doing the following exercise. Ask a practice partner to attack any part of your body at random (but do not allow strikes to the head, neck, or groin). Ask him or her to start slow, building up speed until he or she lands a punch. Then take your turn to try to land a punch.

attack a more vulnerable target than your attacker's arm. You can block using any part of your arms or legs, but it is easiest to block using the forearms.

To perform an inside forearm block, stand in forward stance (see p. 39), with one fist in front of your chest, your elbow bent, and the other fist by your hip. Ask your partner to throw a punch at your head or chest. Drop your arm, and immediately sweep your forearm across the front of your body, like a windshield wiper. Your forearm is long, which means you do not have to be too accurate to parry a blow, but you should aim to have your forearm vertical so that you can deflect your attacker's punch with your wrist. Start slow, building up speed as you feel more confident.

A variation on the inside forearm block is the downward inside-forearm block. This block sweeps your attacker's leg or arm away and downward while he or she is striking at your lower body or legs. To perform this block, stand in forward stance (see p. 39), with one fist in front of your chest, your elbow bent, and the other fist by your hip. Ask your partner to gently punch or kick at your lower body. Sweep your leading arm down to deflect the strike away from your body, leaving your attacker's body open to counterattack.

Deadly Weapons

You may think that the contents of the average purse contains some pretty deadly weapons—a nail file, a perfume atomizer, a can of mace—but these are nothing compared to the weapons that you have unknowingly been carrying with you since birth: your hands, feet, elbows, and knees.

Used properly and against the right targets (see pp. 61–63), a well-placed hand, foot, knee, or elbow can be just as devastating as a knife. The type of natural weapon you use will depend on the target. For example, it would be useless to try and drive your fingers into a thickly muscled or hard-boned area; all you would succeed in doing would be to hurt your own hand. The techniques in this section are drawn from the martial art of karate, which specializes in attacking moves using the body as a weapon.

ARMS AND LEGS AS WEAPONS

One of the most effective bodily weapons is the fist. To make a standard fist, bend your fingers so that they fold over onto themselves. Continue folding until your fingers are pressed tightly in your palm. Clamp the fist across the

In many unarmed fighting styles—Eastern or Western—the hand is the weapon of choice. Highly maneuverable and with many configurations and striking zones, the hand will often be your first resort.

HOW TO MAKE A FIST

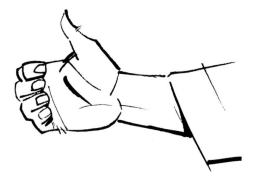

STEP 1: Curl the fingers tightly on themselves, starting from the first and second joints.

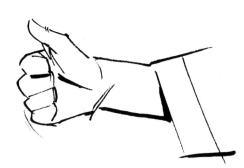

STEP 2: Close the fingers on the palm completely, protecting them from injury.

STEP 3: Finally, clamp the thumb down out of the way onto the first two fingers.

second joint of the index and middle fingers. Make sure that your little finger does not become relaxed and detached from the fist.

FOREFIST STRIKE

With the forefist, the knuckles of the index and middle fingers are used to strike the target. The wrist is held in line with the forearm in order to concentrate the power of the blow. Remember from the kata drills that rotating the fist at the end of the movement will increase its "punch". The forefist is your all-purpose weapon, but it is particularly effective when aimed at the face (avoid hitting the mouth, however, or the teeth will cut you), the throat, or the solar plexus.

The forefist strike is obvious, however, and thus your attacker may be able to avoid it if he or she sees it coming. Less obvious are strikes using the back or side of the fist. The delivery of a blow using these fists

FOREFIST

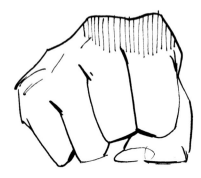

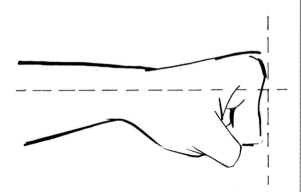

STEP 1: The striking surface of the forefist is the first two knuckles of the hand. Keep the thumb tucked away.

STEP 2: Rotate as you strike, as in the punches, but connect with the target with the fist square on.

STEP 3: Step forward, bringing your hips into play as you strike the opponent in the nose or eye.

STEP 4: The forefist is powerful enough to inflict severe damage to body targets such as the solar plexus.

HAND-SPEAR

STEP 2: With the fingers extended and together, hold the thumb at the base of the fingers.

STEP 3: Strike a taller attacker's eyes with an upper thrust with the hand-spear.

STEP 1: Like in the punch, lead with the right leg if you intend to strike with the right hand.

STEP 4: A blow to the solar plexus has to be accurate to be effective.

involves a snapping motion, and then straightening your bent elbow. The targets for these fists include the eyes, chin, and ribs.

HAND-SPEAR

To make the hand-spear, extend your fingers and hold them together tightly. Fold your thumb and clamp it close to the base of your forefinger. Strike using the tips of the index, middle, and ring fingers, with your arm straight. Targets for the hand-spear include the eyes, the point just below the nose, the ribs, and the solar plexus.

PALM HEEL

To use the heel of the palm as a weapon, flex the hand up as far as it will go,

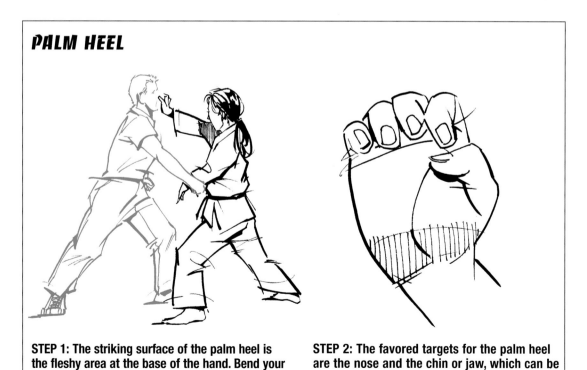

PALM HEEL

STEP 1: The striking surface of the palm heel is the fleshy area at the base of the hand. Bend your fingers and thumb to keep them out of the way.

STEP 2: The favored targets for the palm heel are the nose and the chin or jaw, which can be dislocated by a strong blow.

SWORD HAND

The classic "karate-chop" hand is used on targets such as the neck and ears for maximum effect.

with your palm forward, your fingers curled inward, and your thumb pressed into the base of the index finger. Again, the delivery is the straight line to the target. The classical target for the palm heel is the chin; a well-aimed blow will dislocate an attacker's jaw.

SWORD HAND

Another way to use your hand as a weapon is to make a "sword hand." Press your fingers tightly together, and keep your wrist in a straight line with your forearm and fingers. Clamp the thumb tightly on the palm, but do not over-bend the thumb. Strike your opponent's neck or ear using the bony outer edge of your hand in a classic "karate-chop" motion.

FOREARM BONES

The bony heads of the forearm bones form an extremely hard striking surface. Hook the fingers together to keep them out of the way and strike directly upward. Favored targets include the chin and the armpit. Your blows will also benefit from the element of surprise, as this hand weapon is not used in Western unarmed combat.

ELBOW

STEP 1: Keep the elbow close to the chest as you swing it out.

STEP 2: Use upward strikes against the face or upper body.

STEP 3: Use downward strikes against the back and neck.

BALL OF THE FOOT

STEP 1: Flex the ankle and curl in the toes to expose the ball of the foot.

STEP 2: Use a front kick from the forward stance to strike the upper body.

HEEL OF THE FOOT

STEP 1: Flex the ankle to kick directly back or down.

STEP 2: If grabbed from behind, use the heel on the attacker's instep.

STRIKING WITH THE ELBOW

The following are some striking techniques using the elbow:

- Side strike: Drive your elbow sideways in a straight line to the target. Rotate your wrist at the end of the movement so that your fist finishes palm-down.
- Forward strike: Make an "elbowing-out-of-the-way" motion with your bent arm. You can increase the power of the strike by simultaneously twisting your hips.
- Upward strike: Drive your elbow up and forward, turning the arm in slightly and twisting your hips as you strike.
- Downward strike: Raise your elbow as high as you can, and make a fist with the hand of your striking arm. Strike downwards, turning your arm in slightly and twisting your hips.

ELBOW STRIKES

The elbow is a versatile weapon that can be used in many ways. Bend your arm without locking it in place, to expose the bony point of the elbow joint. The elbow can be used for a quick follow-up blow after you have successfully struck your opponent with your hand. As your attacker is reeling from your first blow, step forward and pursue the advantage with an elbow strike. The targets for the elbow include the neck and the solar plexus. The elbow can be used in combination strikes. If you have struck your opponent in the face with your forefist, swing your arm around to inflict a second strike to his or her face or throat with your elbow, or, if he or she is falling, strike down.

SIDE OF THE FOOT

STEP 1: Flex the ankle inward to strike with the outer edge of the foot.

STEP 2: Deliver a blow to the legs, around your opponent's knee joint, with a side kick.

BALL OF THE FOOT

The ball of the foot can also be an effective weapon. To use it, curl your toes up (to keep them out of harm's way), and flex your ankle as much as possible. Strike using the thick pad of tissue beneath your toes. Be careful when you kick not to strike too high and lose your balance. Unless you are very flexible or have practiced the technique and are confident, keep your kicks low, aiming for the groin and legs of an attacker. (For a kicking technique using the ball of the foot, see the kata section, pp. 49–56).

HEEL OF THE FOOT

For a striking technique using the heel, follow the description given in the kata section (see pp. 49–56). The heel can also be used to stomp on the inside of an attacker's foot. This will cause enough pain for the attacker to release you, allowing you to make your getaway.

SIDE OF THE FOOT

To strike using the side of the foot, follow the description given in the kata section (see pp. 49–56). The best targets for the side of the foot are the knee or the shin. A well-targeted kick to the side of the knee or just below the joint will smash the knee and immobilize your attacker.

KNEE STRIKE

Your legs are the strongest and largest muscles in your body, and a blow from a bent leg exposing the bony protrusion of the kneecap can be a knockout move. Strike at the solar plexus to wind your opponent or at his or her groin. The bony outer edge of the forearm is another potential weapon; it can be used like a staff, to strike your attacker's limbs and face.

THROWS

Throws come in many forms, from simple trips to over-the-shoulder

KNEE

STEP 1: The safest way to use your knee is in a straight upward thrust.

STEP 2: Use the knee to attack the solar plexus or groin.

FOLLOWING UP ON A THROW

If you decide that you must follow up on your throw in order to prevent pursuit or further aggression, do not let go of your attacker once you have thrown him or her. Hold on to an arm to maintain some control and to prevent him or her from rolling out. This will also increase your attacker's chance of making a bad landing. Attack the face or neck directly, as these will be the closest targets in range.

Getting a good grip on someone is essential for the success of a throw. A martial arts suit is made of rip-resistant material, but when going for a grip on street clothes, this may not always be the case.

LEG ASTRIDE THROW

STEP 1: Grab hold of your attacker by his sleeves and collar, if he is wearing a jacket or coat, or by his upper arms if he is not.

STEP 2: Jump forward, with your right foot preventing your attacker's right foot from moving.

STEP 3: Bending forward from the waist, push with your right arm, and pull with your left arm to take him over.

OUTSIDE HOOK THROW

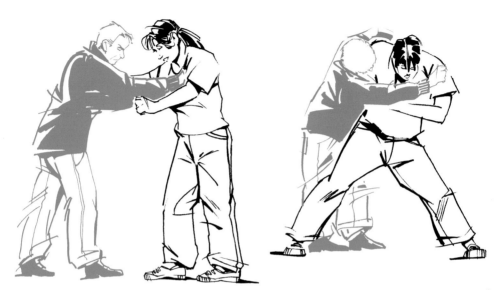

STEP 1: Close in on your attacker, leading with your left foot. Grab hold of his right arm or sleeve with your left hand, and swing your right hand across his throat. Push forward as hard as you can, unbalancing him.

STEP 2: Bring your right foot through and around his right leg and drop it to the floor, pressing your thigh into his.

STEP 3: Sweep backward with your right leg, literally taking your attacker's legs out from under him.

throws, to the up-and-over tumble so beloved of Western movie directors, where one man sits down in front of his opponent, grabs him by the lapels while sticking one foot in his stomach and pulling him forward. The effect is always spectacular on celluloid, but it is not a throw that any beginner should attempt. Unless you have very good timing, you will end up with your attacker exactly where you do not want him or her: right on top of you.

Success in throws of any kind comes from moving toward your attacker rather than away. Thus, you have to overcome your natural desire to run away from an aggressor and actually enter and then take over his or her body

Competition throws in judo and other martial arts can be extremely impressive, with bodies somersaulting through the air, but in real-life situations it's much safer to keep the throws simple and small.

space. Throwing does not depend on size or strength; it is the application of the leverage principle to move your attacker's center of gravity to a point where his or her balance is broken.

HOOK THROW

The simplest type of throw is the hook, in which you wrap your leg around that of your attacker, either from the inside or the outside, while upsetting the upper-body balance with your arms. The trick here, as with all the throws, is to make sure that the attacker does not end up falling on top of you. To avoid this situation, you must not make a half-hearted attempt at a throw; rather, you must throw all your strength and weight into the throw and do it as fast as you can.

Practice throwing with a partner, making sure that both of you are confident with the break-falling techniques. Use padding of some kind on the floor. Initially, you should learn the techniques while standing in one spot.

LOCKS

Most fights consist of an exchange of blows ended by knockout, submission, or flight. However, there may be situations in which you find yourself in need of controlling an attacker. This is where joint locks and chokes come into their own. With a lock, you can cause enough pain to get an attacker to lie meekly down and wait for the police to take him or her away; with a choke, you can put him or her to sleep.

Like any great, yet simple, idea, joint locks are used in all of the world's fighting traditions, from Japan's jujutsu to modern America's World Wrestling Federation (WWF). The idea is to control your opponent through an effective mechanism: pain. To fully understand the principles and applications of the lock—as well as to see how much they hurt—you will need a partner. Do not be too hard on your partner, however. Remember, it is his or her turn next! The way to signal that you have had enough is to tap your partner's body or the floor a couple of times.

The best locks are those that are applied to smaller joints, such as the fingers and wrists; these need much less effort to apply than locks to the shoulder or head, for example. Like throws, the theory of locks is simple, but the practice is much more difficult to apply in a fighting situation.

Locks work because the joint is forced to go in the opposite direction from which it is meant to work, causing instant, excruciating pain. However, applying the lock and maintaining it are another matter. Remember that your attacker has three other limbs free and that he or she may try to punch or kick his or her way out of the lock before you have applied it fully. However, once the lock is truly secure, your attacker will be in too much pain to resist.

The most effective locks are on the smaller joints—fingers or wrists. A well-executed lock can lead to a rapid submission.

FINGER LOCK

To practice the finger lock, have your partner pretend to make a grab for you from the front. Meet his or her hand palm-to-palm. Grab three or four of his or her fingers, and push them

WRIST LOCK

STEP 1: As your attacker moves forward toward you, step in, instead of away, pushing or striking at his arms to keep his hands apart and prevent him from grabbing hold of you.

STEP 2: Grab one of his wrists with both hands and turn the palm so that it faces upward. Press into his hand with both thumbs.

STEP 3: Steady pressure should bring your attacker to his knees. Keep your body out of range of his free arm or leg and maintain the pressure.

toward his or her elbow while pulling the arm down. Keep up the pressure, otherwise your partner will be able to escape. If you have applied the lock correctly, you should be able to take your partner down to the floor.

BACKWARDS FINGER LOCK

Step to the side of your partner, and put your palm on top of his or her hand. Grab his or her index and middle fingers, bending them back toward the elbow. Finally, push the hand behind the back, bringing your partner to the tips of his or her toes.

WRIST LOCK

To practice the wrist lock, stand facing your partner. Ask him or her to reach forward, as if to push you in the chest with his or her right hand. Grab the wrist with both hands, and turn the palm so that it faces upward. Press into the hands with your thumbs. Continue to apply force to the back of the hand until your partner is forced to the ground.

CHOKES

The classic judo and jujutsu chokes interrupt either the air or blood supply to the brain at the neck. It is surprising how little time it takes for a person to pass out when pressure is

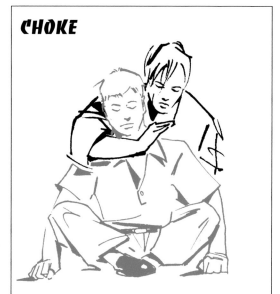

CHOKE

In order to perform a choke, press the bony outside edge of your hand into your attacker's throat. Pull down on the collar of his jacket to increase the pressure.

applied to the neck and throat. When practicing chokes, use the tapping signal to say that you have had enough. This signal will be necessary, as the person being choked will be at a complete loss for words.

When applying a choke, you must maneuver yourself into the right position, which means you will have to get close to your attacker. To practice how to choke from behind, ask your partner to kneel in front of you wearing a sturdy jacket. Place your right hand around the right shoulder and then deep into the jacket collar. Slip your left hand under the other arm, and grab the right side of the jacket. Pull on the jacket, and draw your wrist in.

Be careful not to execute this technique too strongly, or your partner will pass out. If your attacker is not wearing the kind of clothing that you can use in this way, you can just press your wrist into his or her throat.

Glossary

Bout	Free sparring match in the martial arts; these can be no- or full-contact
Chi/qi	Cosmic energy believed by the Chinese to animate all matter; humans acquire chi from food and from the environment; in the soft/internal martial arts, chi is used as a weapon
Dantian	Main reservoir of chi in the human body, located approximately 2 in (5 cm) below the navel
Dojo	Training hall used for all Japanese martial arts
Feng shui	(Chinese: wind and water); art of geomancy in which chi in the environment is manipulated in architecture and interior design to improve health and good luck
Hsing-i	Soft/internal martial art from China which makes use of chi; the movements of hsing-i are based on the trigrams found in the I-Ching
I-Ching	(Book of Changes); a Chinese book of divination and mystical teachings used for fortune telling
Kama	A sickle used in Japanese agriculture
Karate-ka	A student of karate-do; the art of the empty hand
Kata	(Japanese: form); a sequence of exercises used to teach the basic moves of karate-do
Kumite	Non-contact sparring between two martial artists
Kunoichi	Female ninja agent trained in the same skills as her male counterparts

Meridians	Invisible channels in the human body through which the chi flows; each vital organ has its own meridian
Naginata	Japanese medieval weapon consisting of a spear shaft on which is mounted an ax-shaped blade
Ninja	A person trained in ancient Japanese martial arts; formerly employed for espionage and assassinations
Pa-kua	Soft/internal martial art from China, which, unlike t'ai chi ch'uan and hsing-i, makes use of linear movements
Parry	To reduce the force of a blow and redirect it
Qi gung	(Chinese: energy work; also chi kung); techniques designed to increase and control the chi in the body to improve health and fitness
Samurai	Japanese warrior of the feudal period (12th–17th centuries)
Segregation	Separating people on the grounds of race, age, or sex
Tatami	Injury-prevention mats made from woven rice straw
Tonfa	A rice grinder used in Japanese agriculture
Trigram	Symbolic representations of the universe found in the I-Ching; each trigram is made up of full or broken lines and has a distinct meaning

Clothing and Equipment

CLOTHING

Gi: The gi is the most typical martial arts "uniform." Usually in white, but also available in other colors, it consists of a cotton thigh-length jacket and calf-length trousers. Gis come in three weights: light, medium, and heavy. Lightweight gis are cooler than heavyweight gis, but not as strong. The jacket is usually bound at the waist with a belt.

Belt: Belts are used in the martial arts to denote the rank and experience of the wearer. They are made from strong linen or cotton and wrap several times around the body before tying. Beginners usually wear a white belt, and the final belt is almost always black.

Hakama: A long folded skirt with five pleats at the front and one at the back. It is a traditional form of clothing in kendo, iaido, and jujutsu.

Zori: A simple pair of slip-on sandals worn in the dojo when not training to keep the floor clean.

TRAINING AIDS

Mook yan jong: A wooden dummy against which the martial artist practices his blocks and punches and conditions his limbs for combat.

Makiwara: A plank of wood set in the ground used for punching and kicking practice.

Focus pads: Circular pads worn on the hands by one person, while his or her partner uses the pads for training accurate punching.

PROTECTIVE EQUIPMENT

Headguard: A padded, protective helmet that protects the wearer from blows to the face and head.

Joint supports: Tight foam or bandage sleeves that go around elbow, knee, or ankle joints and protect the muscles and joints against damage during training.

Groin protector: A well-padded undergarment for men that protects the testicles and the abdomen from kicks and low punches.

Practice mitts: Lightweight boxing gloves that protect the wearer's hands from damage in sparring, and reduce the risk of cuts being inflicted on the opponent.

Chest protector: A sturdy shield worn by women over the chest to protect the breasts during sparring.

Further Reading

Atkinson, Linda. *Women in the Martial Arts.* New York: Dodd Mead, 1984.

Buller, Debz and Jennifer Lawler. *Kickboxing for Women.* Indiana: Wish Publishing, 2002.

Draeger, Donn F. and Masatoshi Nakayama. *Practical Karate 5: Self-Defense for Women.* Boston: Charles E. Tuttle Co, 1998.

Grosser, Vicky. *Take a Firm Stand: The Young Woman's Guide to Self Defence* (Upstart Series). London: Virago Press, 1993.

Kelljchian, Joseph. *One Woman Every Minute.* Davie, FL: American Bushido, 2000.

Quinn, Kaleghl. *Stand Your Ground: The Self-Defense Guide for Women.* San Francisco: Pandora, 1994.

Redgrave, Raul and Carolyn Seaward. *Self-Defence for Women.* London: Hale, 1983.

Sugano, Jun. *Basic Karate for Women: Health and Self-Defense.* New York: HarperCollins, 1976.

Useful Web Sites

http://www.geocities.com/martialstudents/wmaoi/home.html
http://nwmaf.org/index.shtml
http://www.awmai.org/
http://winstonstableford.com/women.html
http://www.crosswinds.net/~sofia_gr/shotokai/shotokai.htm
http://www.kicks4women.com/
http://www.tuffgrrlz.com/
http://www.apocalypse.org/pub/kiai/

About the Author

Eric Chaline is a personal-training consultant and health and fitness journalist and author with credentials in the martial arts, Zen Buddhism, and yoga. After graduating from Cambridge University and the School of Oriental and African Studies in London, he studied in Japan at Osaka Foreign Studies University, where he pursued his interests in Japanese history, philosophy, and the martial arts. He remained in Japan after completing his studies and supervised the English-language martial arts publications of a major Japanese publisher, which included books on aikido by the current doshu, Ueshiba Morihei, and on kyudo, Japanese archery.

Index

References in italics refer to illustration captions